THE
SASQUATCH
AT
HOME

Henry Kreisel Lecture Series

EDEN ROBINSON

THE SASQUATCH AT HOME

*Traditional Protocols &
Modern Storytelling*

THE UNIVERSITY OF ALBERTA PRESS

Published by

The University of Alberta Press
Ring House 2
Edmonton, Alberta, Canada T6G 2E1

and

Canadian Literature Centre/
Centre de littérature canadienne
3-5 Humanities Centre
University of Alberta
Edmonton, Alberta, Canada T6G 2E5

LIBRARY AND ARCHIVES CANADA
CATALOGUING IN PUBLICATION

Robinson, Eden
    The Sasquatch at home : traditional
protocols & modern storytelling / Eden
Robinson ; introduction by Paula Simons.

(Henry Kreisel memorial lecture series)
Co-published by: Canadian Literature
Centre/Centre de littérature canadienne.
ISBN 978-0-88864-559-3

    1. Robinson, Eden. 2. Robinson, Eden—
Family. 3. Authors, Canadian (English)—
20th century—Biography. 4. Haisla
Indians—British Columbia—Kitimat—
Biography. 5. Storytelling— British
Columbia. I. Canadian Literature Centre
II. Title. III. Series: Henry Kreisel
lecture series ; 4

PS8585.O35143Z78 2011   C813'.54
C2011-900396-1

The University of Alberta Press is
committed to protecting our natural
environment. As part of our efforts, this
book is printed on Enviro Paper: it contains
100% post-consumer recycled fibres and is
acid- and chlorine-free.

The Canadian Literature Centre acknowledges the support of the Alberta
Foundation for the Arts for the Henry
Kreisel Lecture delivered by Eden Robinson
in March 2010 at the University of Alberta.

The University of Alberta Press gratefully
acknowledges the support received for
its publishing program from The Canada
Council for the Arts. The University of
Alberta Press also gratefully acknowledges
the financial support of the Government
of Canada through the Book Publishing
Industry Development Program (BPIDP)
and from the Alberta Foundation for the
Arts for its publishing activities.

FOREWORD

THE KREISEL LECTURES constitute one the most
cherished programs of the Canadian Literature
Centre, established in 2006 in the wake of a leadership
gift by Edmonton's noted bibliophile, Dr. Eric Schloss.
Published within the Kreisel Series, these public annual
lectures set out to ensure Professor Henry Kreisel's legacy,
offering a forum for open, inclusive critical thinking.

Author, University Professor and Officer of the Order
of Canada, Henry Kreisel was born in Vienna into a
Jewish family in 1922. Henry Kreisel left his homeland for
England in 1938 and was interned, in Canada, for eighteen
months during the Second World War. After studying at
the University of Toronto, he began teaching in 1947 at the
University of Alberta and served as Chair of English from
1961 until 1970. He served as Vice-President (Academic)
from 1970 to 1975, and was named University Professor in
1975—the highest scholarly award bestowed on its faculty
members by the University of Alberta. Professor Kreisel
was an inspiring and beloved teacher who taught generations of students to love literature and was one of the
first people to bring the experience of the immigrant to
modern Canadian literature. He died in Edmonton in 1991.

His works include two novels, *The Rich Man* (1948) and *The Betrayal* (1964), and a collection of short stories, *The Almost Meeting* (1981). His internment diary, alongside critical essays on his writing, appears in *Another Country: Writings By and About Henry Kreisel* (1985).

LIMINAIRE

LES CONFÉRENCES KREISEL figurent parmi les
programmes les plus chers du Centre de littérature canadienne, créé en 2006 grâce au don directeur du bibliophile
illustre d'Edmonton, le docteur Eric Schloss. Publiées
dans le cadre de la Série Kreisel, ces conférences publi-
ques et annuelles se consacrent à perpétuer la mémoire de
Monsieur le Professeur Henry Kreisel, offrant un forum
ouvert et inclusif pour la pensée critique.

Auteur, professeur universitaire et Officier de l'Ordre
du Canada, Henry Kreisel naît à Vienne d'une famille
juive en 1922. En 1938, il quitte son pays natal pour
l'Angleterre et est interné pour une durée de dix-huit
mois, au Canada, lors de la Deuxième Guerre mondiale.
Après ses études à l'Université de Toronto, il devient
professeur à l'Université de l'Alberta en 1947, et à partir
de 1961 jusqu'à 1970, il y dirige le département d'anglais.
De 1970 à 1975, il est vice-recteur (universitaire), et il
est nommé professeur hors rang en 1975—la plus haute
distinction scientifique décernée par l'Université de
l'Alberta à un membre de son professorat. Professeur
adoré, il transmet l'amour de la littérature à plusieurs
générations d'étudiants et il est parmi les premiers

écrivains modernes du Canada à aborder l'expérience immigrante. Il décède à Edmonton en 1991. Parmi ses œuvres, on citera les romans, *The Rich Man* (1948) et *The Betrayal* (1964), et un recueil de nouvelles intitulé, *The Almost Meeting* (1981). Son journal d'internement, accompagné d'articles critiques sur son œuvre, paraît dans *Another Country: Writings By and About Henry Kreisel* (1985).

INTRODUCTION

I AM TRULY PROUD and happy to have been invited to introduce Eden Robinson—and to talk to you about two of my favourite western Canadian writers.

First, though, I want to take a moment to thank Eric and Elexis Schloss for their leadership role in making the Canadian Literature Centre and the Kreisel Lectures possible. The Schlosses have, over the years, supported dozens of local worthy charities with their time and their money. But they aren't the kind of philanthropists who just write cheques or organize parties. They have a strong guiding vision of the kind of inclusive, cultured community they'd like to see Edmonton become, and of the national leadership role they'd like to see this city and its academic and arts institutions assume. I know that for Eric Schloss, in particular, the Canadian Literature Centre/le Centre de littérature canadienne, has been a very passionate personal dream—and a dream that has come true. I'd like to salute the Schlosses, not only for their generosity, but for the moral and cultural leadership they consistently offer to our whole community.

Henry Kreisel, of course, was one of our city's most visionary moral and cultural leaders—a gifted writer, an extraordinary teacher, a fine university administrator, and a passionate advocate of new Canadian writers, especially western Canadian writers.

I was lucky enough to have had the privilege of studying with Henry Kreisel near the end of his academic career in the late 1980s, and I found him to be a wonderful mentor: patient, inspiring, deeply learned—not to mention dashingly charming and extremely funny.

He was both a mage and a *mensch*—imagine a Jewish Dumbledore, a sort of secular rabbi, who challenged his students to think, and think hard, about what they read and what they thought. I was truly blessed to have been among the last group of students who had the chance to study with him.

His life story is worthy of its own novel. He was a teenager when he and his family fled Austria in the wake of the Nazi *Anschluss*. They escaped to Britain—but two years later, the young Henry and his father were labelled enemy aliens by the British and sent off to a series internment camps in Québec and New Brunswick.

Instead of being embittered by that experience, when the war was over, Henry Kreisel adopted Canada as his new country; English as his new language; and Edmonton as his new home. As a professor and senior administrator, he played an essential, foundational role in building the University of Alberta into the international university it is today.

He was one of Edmonton's first novelists and short story writers, one of the first to make our city real by writing about a quirky, evolving multicultural boom-city on the edge of the frontier. His stories look simple on the surface, but they're shot through with rich and complex ironies. He was fascinated by the unique mix of people and cultures he found here, inspired and energized by the clash of identities and beliefs he saw around him—and felt within him.

It was, he once wrote, "a constant struggle that one had to accept."

"I began to understand that identity was not something forever fixed or static," he wrote in that same essay, "It was rather like a tree. New branches, new leaves could grow, new roots could be put down, too, but the original roots need not be discarded."

He was the most generous sort of writer—one who loved to discover and celebrate new Canadian talent. I can only imagine how delighted he would have been to meet Eden Robinson.

Like Henry Kreisel, Eden Robinson is also a writer fascinated by roots and leaves, by dislocations, clashes, and cross-pollinations of cultures—in her case, the aboriginal culture of her native British Columbia, and the culture of "mainstream" Canada.

And like Kreisel, who barely escaped the Holocaust and the Nazi death camps, and whose works were often explorations of the nature of human evil, Eden Robinson, too, is an author who isn't afraid to tackle evil head-on. She burst onto the Canadian literary scene in 1996 with her extraordinary short story collection, *Traplines*—a series of four brutal, searing, beautifully crafted and utterly gripping stories about teenagers—both white and aboriginal—growing up in worlds full of abuse and betrayal.

The stories were dark and disturbing indictments of a failed generation of parents—but they were also filled with humour, courage, and even hope. The books won international awards and rave reviews, and established Eden as a fresh, authentic Canadian voice.

Her first novel, *Monkey Beach*, was a more lyrical book, the story of a gifted young woman growing up in an isolated northern native community and coming to terms with her culture, her spiritual heritage, and her gifts. It was a novel that mixed tough social realities with myth and magic and a trickster's wicked sense of humour— a book that told readers more about the hard truths of growing up aboriginal in this country today than a thousand government reports or inquiries, or newspaper stories.

Her latest novel, *Blood Sports*, something of a sequel to *Traplines*, is set instead on the rough streets of East Vancouver—a story of violence, of family loyalty, and of vicious betrayal, of the ties of love and blood that bind us to people, even when we desperately try to break free.

With her first three books, Eden Robinson has not only established herself as one of Canada's most provocative and talented writers—but as a moral and cultural force in her own right.

—PAULA SIMONS

Alone of all the Kwakiutl-speaking tribes the Haisla and Kitlope have a full-fledged maternal exogamic clan organization which is almost identical with that of their Tsimshian neighbors. They say the Haihais and Heiltsuk (Bella Bella) "don't know how to marry" because they originated from a girl who "married" a dog.

— RONALD OLSON
The Social Organization of the Haisla of British Columbia

On the first of July Mr. Mogee retired and Mr. J.E. Rendel succeeded him; but after three days he had a severe heart attack and decided to go to a hospital at his former home, and I was left as his temporary substitute in the Mission and in the post office. Serving as postmaster brought me into much closer contact with the Indians, thus aiding me greatly in the anthropological work; however, it took much time. I was surprised to discover that the Indians carried on a rather extensive correspondence with the department stores in Vancouver, Winnipeg, and Montreal, from which they ordered shoes, clothing of all kinds, tools, instruments, et cetera. The women especially kept me busy ordering dresses, stockings, shoes, jewelry, ribbons, cosmetics, and countless other items.

—IVAN ALEXIS LOPATIN
The Social Life & Religion of the Indians in Kitimat, BC

MY NAME IS EDEN ROBINSON. My mother is
Heiltsuk[1] from Bella Bella and my father is Haisla from
Kitamaat Village, both small reserves on the northwest
coast of British Columbia. My maternal grandmother's
family was originally from Rivers Inlet. Since both sides
of my family are matrilineal, technically, my clan name
should have come from my mother's side and I should
belong to the Eagle Clan. When I was ten years old, my
father's family decided to give me and my sister Beaver
Clan names at a Settlement Feast for a chief of the
Beaver Clan who had died a year earlier.

When a chief died, his body was embalmed in a Terrace
funeral home and then he was brought back to his house
where he lay for at least three days, attended around the
clock by family members or people hired by his family
to keep him safe from harm as he rested in the living
room. Community members paid respects by visiting
him in his home and at his memorial. After the funeral
itself, the Thank You Supper was held for people who had
helped out emotionally, financially and organization-
ally. After a year of planning and preparation, the family
announced the date of the Settlement Feast and finally,

of the headstone moving. Modern feasts are truncated affairs lasting six hours at the most. Much of the dancing has gone but the important dirges are sung, names are distributed and re-distributed to clan members, and people from the community are gifted according to status and involvement with the family. In general, headstone moving is considered an affair of the immediate family and close friends. Space in the graveyard is tight and imposing yourself on the family's grief is considered the height of rudeness.

You aren't supposed to attend a feast or a potlatch without an Indian[2] name and since we were living in Kitamaat Village, my mother, although annoyed, for the sake of convenience agreed to let us become Beaver Clan. My younger sister and I received our names at this Settlement Feast. Towards the end of the evening, we were told to go and line up with other children receiving names. I mostly remember being embarrassed to be standing in front of everyone and having no idea what I was supposed to do. One of my aunts told me if I wanted learn more about my name, I should go visit my grand-mother, my ma-ma-oo.[3]

The next day, we went to Ma-ma-oo's house. She told my sister that her name was Sigadum'na'x, which meant Sent Back Chief Lady. A long time ago, a marriage was arranged between a high-ranking lady from up the line and a Haisla chief. They fell deeply in love. Unfortunately, his other four wives became extremely jealous and kept trying to poison her. He couldn't divorce them because they came from powerful families and insulting them in this way would mean, at the very least, nasty feuds. So despite his feelings, he decided to send his love back to her home to save her life. He couldn't divorce her without causing her shame, so he made her a chief. I've since learned two other versions of the story behind my sister's name, but like this one the best.

"Wow," I said when I heard the story. "What does my name mean?"

"Big lady."

"Um, what else does it mean?"

Ma-ma-oo paused. "Biiiiiig lady."

I paused. Names come loaded with rights and histories. Within the Beaver Clan, the name of The Chief of All Haislas (Jasee) is hotly contested and has started many family quarrels. My father is one of the younger sons of a high-ranking family, so my siblings and I receive noble names, but nothing that garners too much prestige and thus requires extensive feasting or that can get me into too much trouble. Implied in my name, Wiwltx°, therefore, is a high rank as it was obtained through marriage and only given to women of noble birth. I was disappointed in my name, and it had nothing to do with rank: I had story-envy. No heartbroken women were standing beside rivers with their long hair unbound as they sang their sadness to the world. Unfortunately, to change my name I'd have to throw a feast. Putting up a feast is like a cross between organizing a large wedding and a small conference. Family politics aside, the sheer cost will run you $5,000 if you cheap out and just invite the chiefs and gift them to witness your event. But then your name would be marred by your miserliness and people would remember how poorly you'd done things long after you'd died. A real feast starts at $10,000 and goes up very, very quickly.

My aunts also gave my mother a name not long after she'd married my father. My mother had just returned to Bella Bella from residential school in Port Alberni. Meanwhile, in the Village, my father was under pressure from his family to get married. At thirty-three years old, they were worried he was going to be an embarrassing bachelor forever. Ma-ma-oo was trying to arrange a marriage with someone suitable. My father decided to go fishing instead.

My maternal grandmother lived in a house near the docks in Bella Bella. One day my mother was looking out the front picture window when she saw my father coming up the gangplank. According to Gran, Mom said, "That's the man I'm going to marry." Mom's version is that she simply asked if she knew who he was.

They met later that night at a jukebox joint held in a house. My father was a hottie and all the girls wanted to dance with him, but he only wanted to dance with my mother. They were getting along so well, they lost track of time. Back then, the air raid siren left over from a World War II naval base would sound and mark the time when the generator was shut off. The streets went dark. Mom's house was on the other side of the reserve. Dad offered to walk her home.

My father took my mother back to the Village after they were married. Dad's family was upset because Mom was twelve years younger than Dad. She was annoyed that they thought she was too young for Dad and expressed her opinion forcefully. My aunts gifted her with an Indian name so she could attend the feasts in the Village. Mom's new name, Halh.qala.ghum.ne'x, meant Sea Monster Turning the Other Way. Although it lacks the romance of my sister's name, I like the attitude it suggests and hope to inherit it.

⚘ I had been introduced to the concept of *nusa*[4] as a child, but had never really understood it until my trip to Graceland with my mother. In 1997, I received £800 for winning the Royal Society of Literature's Winifred Holtby Memorial Prize. After taxes and currency exchange, it worked out to $2,000 CAD. One of my co-workers at the time suggested I put it into RRSPS or at the very least a GIC, but I had always wanted a black leather couch.[5] I spent a few weeks searching for just the right couch and anxiously awaited its delivery. Once it was in my apartment, it seemed monolithic. And it squeaked. And it felt sticky when it was hot. I returned it the next day, deciding what I really wanted was a tropical vacation.

I flipped through travel magazines, trying to insert myself into the happy, sunny pictures. Overwhelmed by the choices, I phoned my mother. I asked her if she could go anywhere in the world, where would she go?

"Graceland," Mom said.

"Really?"

"I would go in a heartbeat."

I was impressed by her certainty. "Okay."

She laughed and we chatted a bit longer. I spent the rest of the evening surfing the Internet for cheap flights and a passable hotel. There were some incredible deals on flights, but the cheapest ones had multiple connections. Mom hated flying, especially take-offs and landings, so the fewer of those we could get away with the better. The Days Inn at Graceland promised Presley-inspired décor, a guitar-shaped pool and a twenty-four-hour Elvis movie channel. The shoulder season rates were great and it was right beside Graceland, so we wouldn't have to rent a car or grab a cab to get there.

"Hey, how'd you like to spend your birthday in Graceland?" I said.

There was a prolonged silence over the phone. "Are you kidding?"

"I just want to make sure you really want to go because everything's non-refundable."

Another silence. "You're serious."

"Yeah, we've got a couple of options for flights, but I think our best bet is a connection out of Seattle."

"I don't think I can afford that."

I explained about the Royal Society prize money and the black leather couch and the desire to go somewhere I'd never been before.

"That seems like a lot of money," she said.

"Do you want to go to Graceland?"

"Well, yes."

"Then let's go."

Dad wasn't interested in going to Graceland with us, so it was just Mom and me. Dad had his heart set on driving from Kitamaat to the 100th Anniversary of the Klondike Gold Rush in Dawson City. Mom hates driving vacations, so she said she'd save her money for Graceland, which Dad said sounded like a glorified shopping trip. We drove up to Dawson that July in his denim-blue standard Ford F-150, but that is a story for another time.

Mom hadn't travelled much, except to visit her grandchildren in Ontario and her mother in Vancouver. Three weeks before we were scheduled to leave, her fears about flying were not soothed by the infamous crash of SwissAir 111 near Peggy's Cove in Nova Scotia and the near-constant media coverage of the wreckage and grieving relatives.

At that point, a series of hurricanes marched across the Gulf States, causing widespread damage and flooding. I had a shaky grasp of American geography, so trying to convince Mom that our plane would not be blown out of the sky was difficult.

"It's a sign," Mom said.

"It's not a sign."

"We aren't meant to go."

"The tickets are non-refundable."

And then our airline pilots went on strike. Which was probably why the tickets had been dirt cheap. Another airline offered to carry their rival's passengers, but things were still iffy when Mom flew into the Vancouver airport to meet up with me. From her pale complexion and bug-eyed expression, I knew the only things that could have got her on that plane were a) her grandchildren or b) Graceland.

We landed in Memphis at night. The cab ride to the hotel was quiet. We were both exhausted. I think I was expecting a longer ride because the blue billboard announcing our arrival at Graceland seemed abrupt. After dragging our luggage to our room, I asked if she wanted to look around or just pass out.

"I'm going to the gates," Mom said.

We passed an Elvis-themed strip mall called Graceland Plaza. We peered in at the closed stores and then crossed the street. The Manor was lit by floodlights. It seemed smaller than I'd been expecting. A stone wall surrounding it was covered in graffiti left there by fans, who were invited by a sign to use the black Sharpies provided to leave a note or signature. We took pictures of each other, and then other tourists took pictures of us together, looking shell-shocked.

In the morning, we went straight to the ticket counter and bought the Platinum Tour, which included all four Elvis museums and the Manor. Mom wanted to go straight to the Manor. We were given audio headsets, which would guide us through the rooms. I put my headphones on. Mom left hers hanging around her neck, ignoring the flow of traffic and irritated glances as she slowly made her way through the entrance.

I turned my Walkman on and began the tour. Halfway through the first room, I realized Mom wasn't with me. I found her staring at a white bedroom with purple furniture. I was about to explain the headphones to her when I realized she was trembling.

"This is his mother's room," she said.

We spent a week in Memphis, and I got the immersion course in Elvis. But there, at that moment, while Mom was telling me stories about Elvis and his mother,

I was glad we'd come here together. You should not go to Graceland without an Elvis fan. It's like Christmas without kids—you lose that sense of wonder. The Manor wasn't that impressive if you just looked at it as a house. More importantly, as we walked slowly through the house and she touched the walls, everything had a story, a history. In each story was everything she valued and loved and wanted me to remember and carry with me.[6]

This is nusa.

As clear and complete as we want this discussion of

our nuyem to be, it is important to recognize that

the Old People realized that some things

cannot be shared. This was and remains a way

of preserving our culture. In times past, it was

recognized that whatever the missionaries

knew about our culture, they tried to suppress.

The less they knew, the safer our traditions

remained. Nowadays, we simply realize that there

are aspects of our traditional perspective and values

that non-Haislas would never be able to understand.

So this and any public discussion of the nuyem

must be recognized as less complete than it would be

if our grandmother were talking to us.

Still, within those bounds we are trying to be

as explicit as we can be. The elders who have

participated in this effort to describe the nuyem

have all encouraged that we "tell it like it is,

because what we don't get down now

will probably be lost."

—FROM OUR NUYEM SAYS...

A HELICOPTER chops though the low clouds, thumping like a grouse when close, then fading—hollow taps as it traces the tower lines west into the rugged mountains. Logging roads seam the quiltwork patterns of regrowth along the steep sides of the Coast Range that frames the deep waters of the Douglas Channel. Towards the ocean, in The Kitlope Heritage Conservancy, the old-growth forest remains untouched. Beneath the evergreen canopy, the dense moss muffles sound and rain leaks through in heavy drips.

The Kitlope is at the head of the Gardner Canal that leads off from the Douglas Channel, a little over 100 KM from Kitamaat Village, or 120 KM from the town of Kitimat, famous for its aluminum smelter. The name "Kitlope" is a Tsimshian word meaning "people of the rock," a reference to the sheer, grey granite cliffs and peaks that glitter with melting glaciers in the summer and are shrouded with snow in the winter. Hudson's Bay Company officials adopted the current name after it was placed on an Admiralty chart during the survey made by Captain Pender in the *Beaver*.[7] Originally, there were seven villages in the Kitlope. The branch of the Haisla who

lived in the Kitlope called themselves Henaaksiala, "few
people in each village" of the Husduwachsdu "from the
place of the milky blue waters." These glacier-fed rivers
and streams are the spawning ground of all five species of
Pacific salmon, herring and oolichan.

Late in 1918, when the Haisla population was already
struggling with tuberculosis and waves of smallpox, the
Spanish Influenza struck. In less than eight weeks, 10 per
cent of the population died.[8] Hardest hit were children
under the age of six. Burial records kept by missionaries
and birth records from Indian Agents document devas-
tating infant mortality rates and some years in which no
babies were born. Severe population decline had already
led to three separate branches of the Haisla—the Nalabila,
the Xa'isla, and Gildalidox[9]—to winter with each other.
The Henaaksiala, who had once numbered more than all
the other Haisla combined, were reduced to 100 people
from an original population of between 1,000 and 1,200.
After years of steady migration to the main Kitamaat
Mission, the Henaaksiala formally amalgamated with the
Haisla in 1948.[10] They left behind ghost villages that are
slowly dissolving back into the forest.

Yet the tug of tradition continues. Every year, a small group of Haisla people, mainly members descended from Henaaksiala families, return to the Kitlope in early to mid-March and stay there until early April. The ground is covered in snow and often the rivers are frozen. They stop at old village of Kemano, now a row of dilapidated houses along a stony beach. A nearby graveyard is a monument to The Great Dying—a tumble of graves marked by mossy clan crests and crumbling crosses. Some wait here and others continue deeper into the conservancy. At the mouth of the Kitlope River, the boats pause. Each person reaches over the side and, one by one, washes their face. They re-introduce themselves to the living land. They clear away the past so they can see with new eyes.

In all the Haisla origin stories, the Douglas Channel was uninhabited because a great monster lived here. A long time ago, a search party trying to find some lost hunters from what is now called Port Simpson stopped when they saw in the distance a large, white mouth opening and slowly closing.[11] They fled, telling everyone the monster must have eaten the hunters. Most variations of the story have a young man being forced from a village near the head of Oweekeno Lake (Rivers Inlet) because of civil war or being wrongly accused of murder. He and his family fled. They arrived at the entrance of the Douglas Channel and the young man and a handful of his bravest warriors paddled on ahead to investigate. They saw the monster in the distance and stopped, terrified. It didn't seem to notice them and, curiosity aroused, they went closer. What had appeared to be a mouth from a distance was actually a flock of millions of seagulls sitting on sandbars and suddenly rising. They were feeding on a small fish that the men brought back to their people. One of the oldest women cooked it, ate it and promptly took a nap. When she woke, she said it was quite tasty. And so the first Haisla people discovered their new home and oolichans.[12]

Oolichans spend their lives in the Pacific Ocean feeding on plankton.[13] Weak swimmers, they rely on tidal flows to help return to their spawning grounds at the upper tidal reaches of rivers. *Thaleichthys pacificus* (rich fish of the Pacific), as the oolichan is known formally, has 15 per cent oil content. Salmon may be vital to the coastal nations of British Columbia, but oolichans arrived at the end of winter when most stored food supplies were depleted and, in harsh winters, people were facing starvation. Oolichans are eaten fresh, smoked and salted. Oil rendered from oolichans is commonly known as "grease" and was used to preserve food (in the days before refrigeration), as a spread like butter, and as a cure-all.

My father remembers his grandmother telling us stories of early oolichan runs when we were children. In the old days, the chiefs had to give permission to start fishing. They studied the river, the run, and if everything looked good, they gave their okay. Once, Ma-ma-oo told us, Jasee was getting married and in the middle of the ceremony, a man burst into the church and said the oolichan were running. The minister watched as the entire wedding party ran down to the river and waited impatiently for the chief's decision. As soon as he said it was okay, the bride hiked up her wedding gown and waded into the river. Everyone from the flower girl to the grandfather of the bride helped out in his or her wedding finery.

When asked about fishing, my uncle Gordon Robinson said: "The most important fishing operation for the Haisla's was oolichan fishing....From reading a white man's history, you get the impression that the Indians were continually at war. That is a false impression. There was a lot of trade, you lived by trade and you couldn't trade with your enemy."[14]

On the coast where rare materials were symbols of prestige, nothing was more valuable than grease. Chiefs gave away grease at potlatches to prove their wealth, their stature, and their ability to mobilize their large and often fractious families.[15] Once attendees had accepted the gifts, they had accepted the chief's claim. Networks of grease trails with elaborate and well-maintained suspension bridges and canoe routes linked the coast to inland regions, while canoe routes connected coastal people with access to oolichans to people who didn't.

"We can't go without our eulachon oil. We use it in just about everything—fish, herring eggs, dried fish. If we don't have that eulachon oil, we don't feel like eating fish," said Bea Wilson, a Henaaksiala elder in a Museum Note *Eulachon: A Fish to Cure Ḥumanity.*[16]

In 2008, my father and I were on a sandbar off the Prince Rupert highway in British Columbia, dip net fishing for *jak'wun*, the Haisla word for oolichan. We weren't alone. A mass of screeching seagulls dove and rose continuously over the choppy ocean. The gnarled roots of a two-storey-high cedar stump washed onto the bar acted as a perch to both seagulls and a dozen pot-bellied eagles too fat to fish anymore. A pack of seals herded a school of jak'wun to a more convenient snacking location.

Dad paused, leaning on his wooden dip net like it was a staff. He patiently scanned the shore for signs of jak'wun. With his grizzled hair and weather-beaten face, with the snow-capped mountains jutting up behind him and the ocean waves swelling beside him, Dad was strikingly Tolkienesque. I had a white plastic grocery bag over my head and I wore rain clogs and a novelty Christmas sweater I didn't mind getting fish guts on. Windblown sleet numbed my face and made my flared jeans flap sullenly against my calves. Earlier that morning when we'd started off, it was all sunshine and southerly breezes. I pooh-poohed the rain slickers and gumboots Dad tried to foist on me as overly cautious and sweat-inducing.

Out there in the cold and wet, I wished we could sit in our car parked on the shoulder of the highway with the slicker-suited Kitsumkalum and Kitselas locals, who were waiting for a break in the weather, comfortably ensconced in their SUVs and Ford F-150s. When we stopped at the Kitsumkalum Tempo gas station, the attendants recognized the dip net immediately and knew where we were headed. The young native cashier wrinkled her nose and said her granny still ate oolichans but she didn't really care for them. Dad chatted up the gas attendants, trying to find out how the run was going and if anyone was selling fresh oolichans. Dad wanted to try drive up to Canyon City tomorrow if we were skunked today.

None of this driving around would have been necessary if the oolichans were still running in Haisla territory, but they are sensitive fish and won't run if they're too stressed, or if the water is too fast or too warm. The runs near Kitimat were compromised by effluent from the

town of Kitimat, Eurocan Pulp & Paper and Alcan
Aluminum smelters. The runs further down the Douglas
Channel in the Kitlope and Kemano areas have always
been spotty, but had been non-existent recently. We
hadn't had a decent oolichan run in five years, which was
worrying many people, especially the elders. Of course
the fish are a concern, but it's the traditions that go with
the fish that are in real trouble. A couple of families in the
Village still know how to render the oolichan grease, but
the commitment of time and money coupled with the bad
runs has meant that no grease has been made and the
price of the stockpiled grease has shot up to $300 a gallon.
Dad's house was broken into the year before and the big
screen TV and stereo systems and DVD collection were
untouched. The only thing taken was a gallon jar
of grease.

I kept glancing at the road in case someone stomped
down and asked us what the hell we were doing. I was
only reassured we weren't breeching protocol when Dad
wandered back to the road to question the locals about
how long they'd been waiting. He'd played basketball
with one of the elders and they shot the breeze. I went
back to sit in the car and thaw out while listening to Wild
William Wesley on CFNR, the local aboriginal station,
mentally taking notes about the irony of food fishing in
the imperial era of McDonald's. For instance, you have to
fairly well-off to eat traditional Haisla cuisine. Sure, the
fish and game are free, but after factoring in fuel, time,
equipment, and maintenance of various vehicles, it's
cheaper to buy frozen fish from the grocery store than it
is to physically go out and get it.

Morning turned into afternoon and we were still
waiting. Dad loped back to the car with news that
someone was trading oolichans from the Nass Valley for
cigarettes. We drove to a small house near the Terrace
Wal-Mart and Dad struck a deal. We ended up with a
bucket of less than fresh oolichans, but, as Dad said,
resigned, beggars can't be choosers.

When we returned home, the afternoon was already
darkening, but Dad couldn't wait to put the oolichans up
in the smokehouse. He scrubbed off a single *dom*, a thin
cedar stick about four feet long, and showed me how to
thread the dom in through the oolichan's mouth and out
its gills. One dom easily holds thirty small fish.

"Your ma-ma-oo used to put up 500 doms a day all by
herself," he said.

As he told me about the oolichan runs of old, it was
easy to imagine Ma-ma-oo bustling cheerfully though the
smokehouse, making it look effortless. I hate to think of
thousands of years of tradition dying with my generation.
If the oolichans don't return to our rivers, we lose more
than a species. We lose a connection with our history, a
thread of tradition that ties us to this particular piece of
the Earth, that ties our ancestors to our children.

(68) Veratrum viride *Ait. Ssp.* Eschscholzii

(A. Gray) Love & Love

(Indian Hellebore, or False Hellebore)

— (HAISLA) AUX SULI

Medicine: CAUTION; HIGHLY TOXIC.

Respiratory aid; analgesic or anti-inflammatory

(treatment for arthritis and other pain);

hypertension and blood disorder,

unspecified medicine, emetic, purgative,

sedative, hemostat.

Ritual or Spiritual: *ritual medicine (shamanistic*

preparation, purification, emetic, repels ghosts,

illness, evil and witchcraft, acquisition of luck);

used by bear and wolf as ritual medicine.

— BRIAN D. COMPTON
"Upper North Wakashan"

The best known monsters of Haisla territory

were the Bekwis. These were large, hairy

creatures that were reported occasionally in the

Q'waq'waksiyas shoreline area just above

Bishop Bay, and for that reason it is known as

Monkey Beach. These Bekwis have come to be called

Sasquatches or "stick men" elsewhere.

—*OUR HAISLA STEWARDSHIP AREAS*

THE HAISLA measure of intelligence is slightly different from that of mainstream culture. Three main indicators are an ability to trace your family roots back to mythic times, not having to be told twice and being able to replicate an action after being shown how to do it. By most Haisla measurements, I am "special." I can vaguely remember my immediate family and get fuzzy on the stories. Anyone who has taught me (or tried to teach me) Haisla knows you can tell me twenty or so times and I might remember a word or phrase. I have a vague idea of how to live a traditional life but would probably starve if I had to catch and cure my own fish and berries.

I enjoyed school because it was the first place where people considered me smart. I was much better at remembering things that were written down and in learning from books. After high school, I went to the University of Victoria for my Bachelor of Fine Arts and then immediately began grad school at the University of British Columbia for my Master of Fine Arts. I began writing my first novel as my thesis, and then switched to a collection of short stories so that I could use my novel as a grant application for the now defunct Explorations

Program. My thesis became my first short story collection[17] and I immediately began writing my novel, a coming-of-age story set on the northwest coast.

I ran into problems early. First, the main character was a young woman named Karaoke, about whom I'd written in a short story in the collection called "Queen of the North." Karaoke was traumatized by the events of the short story and lay flat on the page. Next I dithered on whether or not to set the novel in Kitamaat Village or to emulate Margaret Laurence and make up a place. I'd kept Karaoke in the Village and it had been an uncomfortable experience. An entire novel seemed daunting. In the end though, the story lost its context and much of its zip when taken out of the Village so I decided to consult with my aunties on the stickier issues, like Haisla copyright.

I knew I couldn't use any of the clan stories—these are owned by either individuals or families and require permission and a feast in order to be published. Informal stories that were in the public domain, such as stories told to teach children our nuyem, could be published—unless they had information people felt uncomfortable sharing with outsiders, such as spiritual or ceremonial content.

I wanted a couple of scenes at a potlatch, but wasn't sure what I'd have to do to have it included in the novel. A cousin of mine said although most traditional people were uncomfortable talking about the potlatch itself, what the people were doing or saying while the potlatch was going on was a different story. It turned out better for the story because I'd had three exposition-heavy pages that were reduced to a quick transitional paragraph, while the tensions between family members and the children playing around them, oblivious, came to the forefront.

In these early stages of writing *Monkey Beach*, I was invited to a Haisla Rediscovery Camp in the Kitlope Valley. The program sought to reconnect Haisla youth with the traditional ways of learning. If I wrote a short piece, I could participate in the program for free. I jumped at the opportunity of a working vacation that would help me nail the locations in the book. The Kitlope Valley is a remote, untouched watershed with glacier-fed rivers and high, bald mountains. The boat ride took three hours and I rode out with the elders and a dendrologist who was recording culturally modified trees. The camp included myself, some researchers, elders, camp cooks and sixteen sixteen-year-old boys. We transferred into a jet boat at the mouth of the Kitlope River because the river was too shallow for the diesel seiner to go up.

In the mornings we split into small groups and travelled the territory, learning our stories and traditional ways of living. We'd gather wild rice on a mud flat or follow animal tracks or learn about the families that had lived here before depopulation from smallpox and flu epidemics forced them to move to the main reserve. In the evening, we did chores, ate dinner and then were supposed to gather around the lakeshore for cultural sharing around a campfire so that we could teach the others in the group what we had learned that day. The boys were keenly feeling the lack of television, and the batteries for their games and Walkmen had died, so most of their cultural sharing involved recreating scenes from the recently released *Wayne's World*. By the end of two weeks, although I hadn't seen the movie yet, I could recite most of the dialogue and plot points.

The Rediscovery Camp heavily influenced the structure and content of *Monkey Beach*. Walking the territory, boating the territory, eating food I'd collected and being immersed in the stories was inspiring. My grandmother character in the book knew a lot about our traditional healing, so I was particularly interested in learning about plants and medicines. One of the elders at the camp was excited that I was interested in the old medicines and was hopeful that I would carry our knowledge to the younger generation. I asked her about oxsuli,[18] a powerful plant more commonly known as Indian Hellebore. I'd been fascinated by it ever since one of my uncles had tried to use it to help his arthritis. He hadn't listened to the instructions for its safe use, and put an entire root bulb in his bath. Within minutes, he was paralysed and had to call his wife for help. She called the ambulance, but the paramedics couldn't lift him out of the tub. The volunteer firefighters were called in. Most of them were my uncle's high school basketball buddies, and they teased him relentlessly about getting stuck in the tub.

The elder offered to show me a place where the oxsuli were just starting to grow back. A shift in the river had wiped out the mud flats that oxsuli prefer. We took a speedboat out to the site and I tied up on shore. Oxsuli grow tall with heart-shaped elliptic leaves. The tiny greenish-yellow flowers droop from the top in tassels. The berries are highly toxic and range from beige to deep red. The oxsuli we found were only knee-high. As she touched a leaf, she told me a story about her grandmother teaching her about oxsuli just as she was teaching me. She bent over further and cleared away some dirt, exposing the root, a stringy orange cluster. I knew the root was used to keep ghosts away and for good luck, but she told me how to use the root to cure headaches.

"You should get to know its energy," she said. "Lean in and study it."

"Okay."

"I'm glad they're growing back here," she said. "They haven't for a long time."

As I leaned in to study the oxsuli, my rubber boots slipped in the mud and I fell on top of it and squashed it.

The elder was quiet as I picked myself up and tried to unsquash the plant.

"Maybe you should stick to writing," she said.

When we got back to the speedboat, we discovered I had not tied it as effectively as I thought and it was floating away on the tide.

"You tied her up," she said. "You swim out to get her."

Glaciers feed the rivers and the water is cold. I have never bathed less in my entire life than when I was at the Rediscovery Camp. I would roll out of my tent in the morning and wander down to the beach. Most of the two weeks were overcast and chilly. The mountains steamed and the mist formed columns that rose up and merged with the clouds. One morning, a great blue heron balanced on a log watching seals roll in Kitlope Lake. The lake is wide and shallow. Orcas sometimes follow the seals up the lake and their tall dorsal fins slice the water as they hunt. When Dad used to trap here, he would watch the Orcas shimmy up the rocks to grab a seal and slide back into the lake.

The Kitlope is also prime bear habitat. At the mouth of the river on the day we arrived, I saw a black bear on the shore eating seaweed. It stuck its nose in the air as we approached, then waddled into the forest. Black bear footprints were seen lacing our camp. They nosed around the meat freezer and left claw marks on nearby trees. I saw a spirit bear for the first time, a yellowish small bear in an abandoned crabapple grove.

I hoped to see my first Sasquatch or at the very least, pick up a few stories. When I was growing up, my mother used to tell us about Tony's place, an abandoned settler's farm near a lagoon on the mainland across from Bella Bella. When they were children, my mother and her siblings used to pick cherries and plums from the orchard. The farm had been abandoned suddenly—breakfast dishes were still laid out, the beds were unmade and clothes still hung from the laundry line. One of my uncles was at the stage when he was fascinated by coins and he went along the line, carefully checking the pockets with shaking hands. My mother asked him who he was afraid would catch him and he said the sasquatches who were rumoured to have attacked the settlement and carried off one of the white women.

My father said the *b'gwus*, as Sasquatch are called in Haisla, had clans and families, their own songs and feasts. In the stories that Ma-ma-oo told him when he was a child, b'gwus meant Wild Man of the Woods, and he thought they might not be ape-like creatures at all, but exiles who had been banned from their villages and had gone to live where they wouldn't be harassed and that it was loneliness and isolation that made them so strange.

The Kitlope is famously home to Sasquatch. The territory bordering on Bella Coola or Nuhalk lands is mountainous and remote. Many of the old stories passed down the generations talk about the elusive b'gwus and their lack of females. They would creep into villages and steal women who took their fancy. The last encounter was in Miskusa, across from Kemano in 1918. Billy Hall shot and killed one by mistake, thinking it was a bear.[19] After escaping from the other b'gwus, Billy Hall gained special powers and had a mask carved to commemorate the event. Dad had known Billy Hall when he was a child and had an insatiable curiosity about Sasquatches for the rest of his life. He sought out elders and listened to their stories, committing them to memory. He was delighted when I told him I would be writing about Monkey Beach and more enthusiastic than I was to get me to the sites he knew so well.

Ma-ma-oo had a bentwood box full of traditional regalia that was only supposed to be brought out for feasts and potlatches. My father liked to bring the b'gwus mask out and tell us the story of Billy Hall. The b'gwus mask has a dance at the feasts, usually the less formal ones. They were always my favourite part of an otherwise stuffy occasion when I was growing up. All the other dances were serious and you had to be still and pay respectful attention. But when a dancer wears a Sasquatch mask and pretends to dig for clams and cockles, hiding his face shyly,

the children push to the front to watch him. Then he'll spot
a pretty woman in the audience and "abduct" her. For
example, when Iona Campagnolo was with the Liberal
Party, she was an honoured guest at the opening of the
Haisla Recreation Centre. During the ceremonies, the
Sasquatch dancer stopped dead when he saw her, patted
his heart and pretended to drag her off, much to the delight
of the audience.

꙳ A few years later, I made it back to Monkey Beach. I'd
been close at the Rediscovery Camp, but we hadn't had the
time to visit. Since then, I had been holed up in my apart-
ment in Vancouver. I was having difficulty ending the
book and was in search of inspiration. When I asked Dad
if he could take me there for a little research, he enthusiastically agreed—after all, he said, any book that had a
Sasquatch was bound to be a bestseller.

I flew home for a week and caught up with my family.
My main character zipped around in a twelve-foot speedboat with a putt-putt motor, and I had my heart set on
doing the same. The weather wasn't co-operating though.
The wind was fierce and Dad shook his head and told
me we probably wouldn't be going. One of my younger
cousins invited me to a house party. In an attempt not to
appear stodgy, I drank a little too enthusiastically. When
Dad shook me awake early the next morning, he said it
was now or never.

I followed my father to our speedboat. The early
morning air was still and cold but the sky was cloudless,
promising a hot, summer day. Dad jumped down into the
boat and I handed him my bags. He paused in the middle
of loading.

"Do you hear that? That's *gunesella*. When an eagle makes that sound before you go hunting or fishing, it's good luck."

The unseen eagle made a trilling sound, a musical gargling.

I waited for it to appear, watching the trees behind the darkened houses that lined the semicircle of the bay. I knew I should pull out my black notebook and write this down, but I was too hungover and tired to make the effort.

The outboard motor was cranky, and Dad pulled the cord over and over before it decided to start. He cast us off. My stomach rolled. I hunched into my seat and belatedly realized that I'd left my Gravol on the kitchen counter.

I looked back as we pulled out of the bay. The Village was squashed up against the mountains and the water. Kitamaat is home to about 700 members of the Haisla nation. About 800 more live off-reserve. We're almost back to our pre-Contact population of 2,000. Even with the people we have, the housing shortage is acute. New subdivisions have expanded almost to the boundaries of the reserve.

The speedboat skipped across the Douglas Channel. We're seventy miles from the open ocean. The mountains enclose the channel on either side, steep walls of trees and rocks. The shore is a thick brown line against the green of the trees and the dark, dark blue of the channel.

It took us two hours to get to Monkey Beach. When he stopped the motor and oared us ashore, I was disappointed. My childhood memories made it seem much larger than this tiny cove. I noted the whiteness of the sand, made up, he tells me, of ground-up shells. I wandered around, swatting away mosquitoes, horseflies and no-see-ums. Dad pulled out his camcorder.

My brother had told me about a white man who brought gorillas to the Douglas Channel and they escaped, and terrorized people until the winter killed them off. I asked Dad if that's why it's called Monkey Beach. He shook his head. "The Haisla name is Awamusdis, the beach of plenty. There's three different kind of clams and two different kind of cockles. We used to use this beach like our freezer in the winter. Sasquatches dig for cockles here. It's their favourite food."

Long ago, he told me, some Haisla people were camping on the beach. When they woke up, the sacks of cockles they'd collected were emptied, the shells sucked clean. Footprints, large and strange, trailed into the woods. That night, they heard it, a howl not quite wolf, not quite human.

"You don't see them around any more. Some people say they're extinct," Dad said. "But they're not. They're up in the mountains somewhere, and they've built a mall and they're too busy driving around and shopping to visit us anymore."

"Where do you dig for clams and cockles?" I asked, ignoring the jibe.

"Around the point," he said, "the south side of the beach."

My running shoes sank into the soft sand as I made my way to the other side of the beach. I clambered over logs. The sand gave way to slippery, barnacle-covered rocks.

Ah, I thought, when I reached the point. The rest of the beach stretched away until it disappeared behind another point. The tide was too high to reach the south side. I stopped, shivering, excited, already rewriting scenes in my head: Morning light slanted over the mountains as a raven croaks in the trees. An otter bobbed in the kelp, rolled lazily onto its back, then watched me with its hands folded over its belly. A weasel slithered through the logs and hurried into the trees. I took my disposable panoramic camera out of my pocket and began snapping pictures. Dad joined me and I took a photograph of him videotaping me.

We spent the day wandering around the area. I could point to any mountain, any river or any rocky shoreline and he knew the history. Dad especially liked to retell the story of T'ismista, the man who turned to stone. When you are on Kitlope Lake, looking up at the mountain, there is a looming, dark stone figure looking back down at you. That was Henkwa. He lived up on the flats at the top of the lake. One day he called his two dogs to his canoe and started paddling. He went past the bluff that was the place where the Henaaksiala taught their young men to "master the mountains" so they could climb up to get goats. He passed Ago'yewa on the other side of the lake, to the place where the Rediscovery Camp was in 1996. He went a little further and then turned and crossed the lake, beaching his canoe on the east side of the lake just below Ago'yewa. When he got out of the canoe, he left a footprint in the rock on the beach. The footprint is large and easily seen. You can also see the dog prints and the thin line of his spear dragging on the ground beside him. When he climbed up the mountain, he got stuck on one of the steep cliff edges and froze. He couldn't go up and he couldn't go down. In the end, he turned to stone. If you follow his trail up to visit him, be careful. Many people puke blood or get sick and it is rumoured to be bad luck to go too near him. A helicopter tour trying to take pictures of him crashed into Kitlope Lake once....

When Dad was fishing in Kemano, he had been hired by an elder to take them out on the land while she gave nusa to a young hereditary chief, her grandson. As part of his training he was supposed to know his land and all the stories, the history of his clan, his villages and their neighbours. They'd spent days doing exactly what we were doing, bumping around in a small boat. Dad told me stories that she had told her grandson as I scribbled them down in my notebook. My favourite is the one where clams have black tongues because in the beginning, the world was on fire and they tried to put it out by spitting.

As we got ready to leave, I said, "No hungry Sasquatches here today."

"They must be at home," Dad says with a smile, "writing."

NOTES

1. The Heiltsuk Nation's main reserve is Waglisla, BC, which is more commonly referred to as Bella Bella, the name given it by Spanish explorers. Kitamaat Village is known by its residents simply as the Village and was at first a winter camp and, later, a Methodist mission. It is currently the main reserve for the Haisla Nation. The reserve is also referred to as C'imotsa, "snag beach," because of all the stumps and logs that decorate the waterfront.

2. Indian, aboriginal, First Nations, native Canadian are used interchangeably in the context of this essay and most of my work.

3. Pronounced *ma-MAH-ew*.

4. *Nusa*: the traditional way of teaching children Haisla *nuyem*, or protocols.

5. I don't know why. I think it's because when I was a child, having a black leather couch was like wearing red lipstick or smoking skinny cigarettes—somehow it transformed you into a sophisticated grown-up.

6. To commemorate our trip, I wrote in a scene in *Monkey Beach* where my character took off for Graceland when he found out Elvis died.

7. Lopatin, Ivan Alexis. *The Social Life & Religion of the Indians in Kitimat, BC*, Social Science Series, No. 26. Los Angeles: University of Southern California Press, 1945.

8. Pritchard, John C. "Economic Development and the Disintegration of Traditional Culture among the Haisla," PHD thesis, University of British Columbia, 1977.

9. I use Xa'isla to distinguish between the original branch that "lived at the mouth of the river" and the more anglicized "Haisla" as the general term for our nation, although they're both pronounced the same way.

10. Davis, Alison and Wilson, Beatrice. *Salmonberry Blossoms in the New Year: Some Culturally Significant Plants of the Haisla known to occur within the Greater Kitlope Ecosystem.* Kitamaat Village Council, 1995.

11. Robinson, Gordon. *Tales of Kitamaat.* Kitimat, BC: Northern Sentinel Press, 1956.

12. There are over twelve regional spellings of "oolichan" (ooligan, hooligan, ulichan, eulachon, etc.) which is originally a word from a coastal trading language called Chinook. I chose the variation most commonly used by the Haisla.

13. Wilson, Lyle and Allen Drake. *Eulachon: A Fish to Cure Humanity.* Museum Note No. 32. Vancouver: UBC Museum of Anthropology, 1992.

14. Interview with Gordon Robinson on August 2, 1995. Kitamaat Village Council Traditional Use Study, recorded by Allison Davis, Elaine Stewart and Elaine Ross.

15. Potlatch, a Chinook word meaning "to give." A feast with ceremonies and dances held to confirm a chief's authority, consolidate marriages, give new names or mourn a noble man or lady.

16. Wilson and Drake. *Eulachon.*

17. *Traplines* the thesis is almost identical to *Traplines* the collection, except for the omission of a story called "Terminal Avenue," my aboriginal sci-fi bondage response to the Oka Crisis and the Fraser River salmon wars. My editors at the time felt it did not fit the style of the collection as a whole. In its place, we put "Queen of the North."

18. 'o'x° suli.

19. Lopatin, Ivan Alexis. *The Social Life & Religion of the Indians in Kitimat, BC.* Social Science Series, No. 26. Los Angeles: University of Southern California Press, 1945.

RESOURCE MATERIAL FOR THE CURIOUS

Compton, Brian D. "Upper North Wakashan and Southern Tsimshian
  Ethnobotany: The Knowledge and Usage of Plants and Fungi among
  the Oweekeno, Hanaksiala (Kitlope and Kemano), Haisla (Kitamaat)
  and Kitasoo People of the Central and North Coasts of British
  Columbia." PHD diss., University of British Columbia. 1993.

   *Packed with stories. An insane amount of linguistic, ethobotanical and
   comparative northwest coast cultural material in a little less than five
   hundred pages. If you are an avid ethnobotanist or can't find a copy of*
   Salmonberry Blossoms in the New Year, *this is the thesis for you. I
   wish I'd known it existed when I was writing* Monkey Beach.

Davis, Alison and Beatrice Wilson. *Salmonberry Blossoms in the New Year:
  Some Culturally Significant Plants of the Haisla known to occur within
  the Greater Kitlope Ecosystem.* Kitimaat Village, BC: Kitamaat Village
  Council. 1995.

   *The Nanakila Press was created by the Kitamaat Village Council to
   publish material about Haisla culture and territory. Unfortunately,
   shortly after publication of this book, distribution was halted because
   of copyright disputes—which families owned which stories and what
   was appropriate to tell outsiders. The press folded. The book itself is a
   treasure. I referred to it extensively when writing* Monkey Beach. *Alison
   Davis was an ethnobotany student at the University of Victoria when
   I met her at the Rediscovery Camp in the Kitlope and Bea Wilson is a*

well-respected and charming elder from the Kitlope who is absolutely
passionate about its preservation.

Lopatin, Ivan Alexis. *The Social Life & Religion of the Indians in Kitimat, BC.*
Social Science Series, No. 26. Los Angeles: University of Southern
California Press. 1945.

*Russian anthropologist Ivan Lopatin did fieldwork in Kitimat from May
22 until September 20, 1930. His principal informants were Edward Grey
and Christopher Walker. He also spoke with other Kitamaat Village residents and with many of the non-native residents such as the Miss A.M.
Andrews, a nurse in Kitimaat Village and with Reverend Raley who was
the principal of Coqualeetza Institute in Sardis, but who had lived in
Kitamaat Village for over ten years.*

*Lopatin collected information on the Haisla for the National Museum
of Canada. His original papers are currently held in the Canadian
Museum of Civilization in Ottawa: (VII-E-5M), Box 45 f1, f2; (VII-E-6M),
Box 45, f3.*

Olson, Ronald Leroy. *The Social Organization of the Haisla of British
Columbia.* Berkeley: University of California Press. 1940.

*American cultural anthropologist Olson served as a marine in World
War I. In 1931 he became an assistant professor at the University of
California, where his primary interests were the Haisla and the Tlingit
of southeastern Alaska.*

*In the summer of 1935, Olson did fieldwork in Kitimat and Rivers
Inlet where many Haisla were employed in the commercial fish industry.
His chief informants were Chris Walker, Andrew Green, Jonah Howard,
Isaac Woods and Mrs. William Grant.*

*Olson's three volumes of original field notes are held at the Bancroft
Library in the University of California, Berkeley.*

Olson, Ronald. Haisla (Kwakiutl) Field Notes. 3 notebooks, Ethnological
Documents Collection of the Department and Museum of
Anthropology, Brancroft Library, University of California. Reel 113,
251pp plus genealogical charts.

Olson, Ronald. Kitlope-Keemano (Kwakiutl) Field Notes. 1 notebook,
Ethnological Documents Collection of the Department and Museum
of Anthropology, Bancroft Library, University of California.
Reel 114, 17pp.

The field notes are a continuation of the work described in Social
Organization of the Haisla.

Our Haisla Stewardship Areas and *Our Nuyem Says...Our traditional
narratives and values as told by the chiefs and elders of the Haisla
People.* Unpublished typescripts compiled from archival records
and accounts of the Haisla elders by Jay Powell. Prepared by the
Kitamaat Village Council for the Haisla People. Edited by Louise
Barbetti, Tom Robinson, John R. Wilson, and Ken Hall, 2005. Haisla
Treaty Archives at Kitamaat Village Council.

*I was an archival assistant in the Haisla Treaty department for a year
and a half. Part of my job was to sort through random banker boxes that
people from the Kitamaat Village Council would bring in and weed out
the travel expenses from the rare finds—reports on archaeological find-
ings about Old Town, a list of everyone in the Village who owned a car
in 1973, a traditional use study where people were interviewed about
their fishing experiences in the first salmon canneries in our territory.
I hadn't been in the Village when these two unpublished booklets were
distributed and was delighted to find them. My supervisor was the man
who compiled them, Jay Powell—a retired anthropology and linguistics
professor who, in addition to doing research and writing reports for the
Council, also taught Quileute, lectured on cruise lines to Alaska and
spent time in his condo in Mexico.*

Pritchard, John C. "Economic Development and the Disintegration of
Traditional Culture among the Haisla." PHD diss., University of
British Columbia. 1977.

*Touches on most of the primary sources available for those who want to
learn more about economic and political changes that the Haisla culture
survived. Pritchard also wrote one of the first land use and occupancy
studies for the Kitamaat Village Council in the early 1980s.*

Raley, G.H. Papers, BC Archives.

> *George Henry Raley was a Methodist missionary who was posted in the Kitamaat Mission in 1893 and Port Simpson in 1906. Raley took charge of The Coqualeetza Methodist School in Sardis 1914 and remained as principal until his retirement in 1934.*
>
> *In a decade at Kitamaat, he published a well-circulated quarterly newspaper called the Na-Na-Kwa, established a mail service, founded a temperance society, and amassed a large collection of early First Nations materials.*
>
> *In November 1948, more than 600 objects from Raley's collection— acquired largely in Kitamaat and Port Simpson—were purchased by Museum of Anthropology at the University of British Columbia.*

Robinson, Gordon. *Our Tribal Land: Who are the Haisla?* Kitamaat Village Council. Souvenir prepared for the Haisla Homecoming of Land, Boundaries and Legends of the Haisla. 1983.

Robinson, Gordon. *Tales of Kitamaat.* Kitimat: Northern Sentinel Press. 1956.

> *Gordon Robinson was my uncle and the first real person I'd known to have his work published. He attended the Coqualeetza Institute in Sardis and returned to Kitamaat where he taught for five years. In 1949, he became assistant superintendent of the Kwakiutl Indian Agency at Alert Bay, but in 1950, returned to Kitamaat to work for the Aluminum Company of Canada (Alcan). He was chief councillor of Kitamaat Village from 1950–1954.*

Robinson, George. Notebook 1910—Alert Bay and Kitimaat. Newcombe Papers, Add Mss 1077, vol.36, file 8, British Columbia Archives and Records Service.

> *George Robinson was my great-grandfather. He immigrated to Canada from England. He planned to make his fortune and then return to England and finish his education, but in his travels became a member of the Methodist church. He spent some time in Victoria and Haida Gwaii before arriving at the Kitamaat Mission. He spoke Haisla fluently, married my*

---

great-grandmother Kate Starr and operated a general store. He was often used a translator and many of the government documents such as the 1913 Royal Commission on Indian Affairs for the Province of British Columbia (a.k.a. The McKenna-McBride Commission) mention him.

Wilson, Lyle. Collection, Canadian Museum of Civilization, Ottawa. Manuscript on the Haisla, (VII-E-34M), Box 14, f10.

Wilson, Lyle and Allen Drake. *Eulachon: A Fish to Cure Humanity*. Museum Note No. 32. Vancouver: UBC Museum of Anthropology. 1992.

My cousin Lyle Wilson, a renowned Haisla artist, was born in 1955 at Butedale Cannery. He did not pursue art as a possible profession until he attended the University of British Columbia. He has been the Artist in Residence at the Museum of Anthropology for twenty years. The manuscript at the Museum of Civilization details the Haisla artefacts in the collection. The museum note published by the Museum of Anthropology touches on the role of oolichan (a small, smelt-like fish) in northwest coast culture.

HENRY KREISEL LECTURE SERIES

From Mushkegowuk to New Orleans
A Mixed Blood Highway
JOSEPH BOYDEN
ISBN 978-1-897126-29-5

The Old Lost Land of Newfoundland
Family, Memory, Fiction, and Myth
WAYNE JOHNSTON
ISBN 978-1-897126-35-6

Un art de vivre par temps de catastrophe
DANY LAFERRIÈRE
ISBN 978-0-88864-553-1

The Sasquatch at Home
Traditional Protocols & Modern Storytelling
EDEN ROBINSON
ISBN 978-0-88864-559-3

Imagining Ancient Women
ANNABEL LYON
Coming 2012